Tie-Dye

The How-To Book

Virginia Gleser

Book Publishing Co.
Summertown, Tennessee

© 1999 Virginia Gleser

Photography by Don Schneider
Interior design by Warren C. Jefferson

Printed in the U.S. by
    Book Publishing Company
    P.O. Box 99
    Summertown, TN 38483
    1-888-260-8458

ISBN 13 978-1-57067-071-8

ISBN 10 1-57067-071-4

12 11 10 09 08 07 06   3 4 5 6 7 8 9

Gleser, Virginia
        Tie-dye : the how-to book / Virginia Gleser
                p. cm.
        Includes bibliographical references (p.).
        ISBN 1-57067-071-4 (alk. paper)
        1. Tie-dyeing. I. Title
    TT853.5.G584   1999
    746.6'64--dc21   98-51405
                                              CIP

The loving relationship that my husband Robert and I have shared for twenty-eight years has been the foundation of all of my creative endeavors. When my tie-dye business outgrew the garage, he built me a studio. When we outgrew that, he built a larger one. He's in charge of marketing, editing, remodeling, washing machine repair, vehicle maintenance, and taking out the trash as well as running his own business. Somehow he found time for his most important endeavor, raising our six children. His devotion to our family has been my inspiration. To him, I dedicate this book.

Acknowledgements

Many people have helped me in writing this book, and I wish to thank everyone for their support and encouragement. Our customers' and patrons' interest and avid enthusiasm has been the inspiration for this book. Many have become part of our extended family.

The craft show family of artists is a constant source of strength and community. The craft fair promoters who put on such wonderful shows are especially appreciated.

Thanks to my parents Paul and Sophie Crane and my sister Tish Rainey for helping us with the editing. Linda Rake, Stacey Kerr, Kristan Levin, and Terry McGuffin have also helped with the editing and have been close friends for many years.

Don Schneider has done a wonderful job of photographing my work, insisting on good results. He is an artist of photography and photographing my artwork was a challenge to which he skillfully rose.

I want to thank Rhonda Chapman, Sia Lo, Elaine Wright, Choo Thao, Mike Yang, Bla Thao, Roshni Naidu, Susie Chang, Fay Hendrickson, and many others for their skillful help and artistic camaraderie.

Special thanks to Cynthia and Bob Holzapfel and Warren Jefferson at the Book Publishing Company for their help getting this revised edition printed.

My six children, Brian, Eugene, Saul, Audrey, Rosie, and Olivia, are not only inspirational, but became part of our business as well. They would get up at ungodly hours to do shows with us and gave up many weekends and summer weeks. They immersed themselves in the endeavor with a sense of humor and their wonderful energy and interest. They helped make hard work and long hours into a good time.

Table of Contents

About the author

In 1950, when North Korea invaded the South, my missionary parents evacuated to Osaka, Japan, where I was born. We returned to our home in South Korea in 1953, where I was raised with many oriental influences.

The Korean people dress their children in bright primary colors, and when I was young, my Korean dress was a bright red and green, with rainbow-colored stripes on the sleeves. When I was in elementary school in Seoul, I had the opportunity to take dance lessons from a famous Korean traditional dance teacher. The costumes we wore were full-length, beautifully colored dresses. The keen sense of color that is a part of Korean and Japanese culture has inspired me throughout my life.

As a girl, I always wanted to be an artist like my grandmother, Florence Hedelston Crane, who was known for her floral and landscape watercolors. My favorite childhood memories were of visiting my grandmother. She would let me paint with her "palette of one hundred colors," taught me how to mix colors, create shadows, and draw in perspective. I also learned about artistic license, where an artist can alter and balance a picture to make it look right, even though it isn't exactly how it appears in reality. She never went anywhere without her sketch pad and always returned home from a trip with new material to paint.

I moved to the United States to attend college at the age of seventeen. There I studied art, my favorite project being a batik picture. I spent many nights working in the studio to create a multi-colored design with five different overlays of wax and dyes.

In the winter of 1969 I moved to San Francisco, California. The anti-war movement was going strong, and the hippie experience was evolving from dancing in the streets and taking drugs to the commune scene. A large group of young people were trying to figure out if this new lifestyle could make living feel more relevant. Could we survive, raise children, and create a community with some of our idealistic beliefs intact? Could we exist in peace with each other and our environment? People gathered every Monday night at an old ballroom called The Family Dog near the beach in San Francisco. Discussions flourished about every facet of life. Stephen Gaskin, who had been a professor at San Francisco State College, was the leader of the meetings and would steer the dialogue so that our many questions could be raised and answers explored.

Stephen was invited on a lecture tour around the country to various colleges and churches. He was going to adjourn the "Monday Night Class." However many people from the class wanted to go with him to carry the message of peace and love across the country. On Columbus Day, 1970, about 200 people in 70 buses and vans started out on a new discovery of America.

My husband Robert and I, with some other people who wanted to go on this adventure, fixed up an old bus and joined the caravan. The trip took us across the West. At one of our stops in Yellowstone National Park, I received a vision that would later shape my life. Standing alone under the clear, starry night sky, I saw that I was one of a group of Native American women weaving cloth of many beautiful colors and intricate designs. At the time I was wearing a brightly colored skirt woven in Native American patterns, and I realized that I was connected to this land. As an artist, I would honor the Great Spirit. I kept this vision close to my heart, even though it took many years to manifest into reality.

The caravan wandered across the United States visiting New York, Philadelphia, and Washington, D. C., headed south and west by way of Atlanta, Nashville, and Tulsa, finally returning to California. By the time we reached the Pacific, many more people and vehicles had joined our group. It had been a peaceful and exciting trip, but it was over. What were we going to do now? Along the way, we had grown close and had emerged as a tribe or a "village on wheels." People helped each other; those who had money paid for gas and food. There were mechanics who fixed the buses, and there were midwives who delivered the babies. Nobody wanted to break up and go separate ways. We pooled our resources, boarded our buses and vans once more, and moved across the country to settle in rural Tennessee. There, these 21st century pioneers bought some land and founded the intentional spiritual community called The Farm. For the next twelve years, Robert and I lived the great hippie experiment and began raising our six children.

In 1978 we moved to Miami, Florida, to help with Plenty, the Farm's world relief program. Plenty had projects in

Guatemala, Africa, the Caribbean, and Native American lands of South Dakota. In Miami we took care of physically challenged people and senior citizens. We also supported a forty-member crew in Guatemala which helped rebuild a town destroyed by the 1976 earthquake. The project helped bring water to the village and set up a soy dairy.

While we were living in Florida, several women got together in the evenings and had tie-dye parties. We tie-dyed our families' clothes as well as household items. We had fun sharing our knowledge and trying new designs, folds, and color combinations. The children loved the next day when we untied and opened our work. It was like opening presents at Christmas time.

When we ran out of old clothes to experiment with, we bought new T-shirts to work our magic on. We gave them as gifts to friends and relatives. Then friends of friends started asking if they could have tie-dyed T-shirts too. We decided to start making some for sale. A friend of mine, Lori Young, and I asked our husbands if they would watch the children one day a week so we could dye without our two-year-olds getting their fingers into the dyes.

At that time, the men were roofing sub-contractors. We promised them that we would make enough money for them to take the day off. They were skeptical but gave us a chance. We tied the shirts during our kids' nap times twice a week and built up a batch to dye on Wednesdays. The men would take the kids to the beach, the park, or the science museum, and we would dye our hearts out.

We enjoyed our work and loved the next day when we

would open the shirts up and "ooh" and "aah" over the new designs we had created. During our critique sessions, we would talk over changes in color and design. For example, the spiral needed to be placed higher so it was not centered over the belly button, the orange was too strong, the yellow was swallowed up by the blue, the red wasn't squeezed in enough, and so on. The artistic debate continued until we were satisfied with our art.

Tie-dye is a trial-and-error skill. The more we tried new folds and used new color combinations, the prettier the work turned out. And it sold! This was very satisfying.

We took the shirts to stores that would allow us to consign them. Both children's and adult stores reordered. We took our clothing to a farmer's market in Coconut Grove and sold many shirts. The income was taking up the financial slack and the guys didn't mind that. They even enjoyed doing some of the selling.

In 1983 our family left The Farm and resettled in California. We wanted a change and we left with our six children in an old station wagon with enough money to rent a house and get started again.

Robert was employed immediately as a roofer, and I borrowed $60 from his early paychecks to buy a dozen T-shirts and some dye. I was in business again, . . . this time in my garage, on my own, in California.

I tied when my baby was taking her naps and the other children were in school. I would dye one day a week. Robert took the shirts to several stores. "Tie-dye is out, didn't you know, even on Haight Street in San Francisco," was the response. He asked if they would take a dozen shirts on consignment. We would come back in a month and pick them up if they hadn't sold. In two weeks they were sold out, and the stores wanted more.

After that we didn't have to consign them. We bought a used washing machine for $85, and the money I made went back into buying more dye and shirts.

That fall we signed up for an Octoberfest craft fair in a little gold rush town in the Sierra foothills called Murphys. We were so excited. The whole family went to our first craft fair in the old station wagon with a table and a few bags of tie-dyed shirts. People walked by and said, "Is that tie-dye?" or "What is that?" or "Look at the bright colors!" We came home with almost $300, and we were thrilled.

With our six children helping us, we have built Harmony Enterprises. We purchased and remodeled some buildings in the commercial part of town and built our studio and store. Some of the kids added remodeling skills to their small-business education. More than a decade later Harmony Enterprises continues to allow me to develop my artistic skills. It's been a satisfying journey helping to establish tie-dye as a respected American art form.

ntroduction

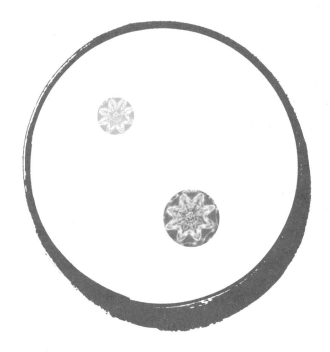

At every craft show (26 in 1998), we are asked "How do you do tie-dye?" Usually the requests are from school-aged kids, accompanied by their supportive parents wanting to do a "cool" project. For the last fifteen years our response to this request has been to sell dye kits. (See Sources, page 90). These kits feature Procion® dyes and a brief introduction to dyeing. Along with the kit we also warned parents that tie-dyeing can be quite a production. Most things that come in contact with the dyes get stained (actually dyed), including plastic containers, floors, clothing, and skin.

Everyone should wear rubber gloves whenever handling dyes and use a dust mask when mixing dye powder. This warning usually discourages some people, but those who stick with it take their dye kits home and "do their thing." Many return wanting to know more: more ties, more dyeing techniques, more, . . . but showtime is not really the time or the place to give instructions. Now comes the book to answer questions about tie-dyeing and help the budding artist along.

ie-Dye Back by Popular Demand

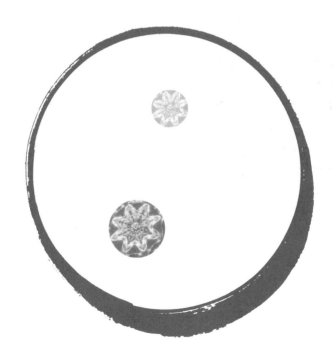

Tie-dyed clothing has once again exploded onto the marketplace. At almost every festive occasion, one can spot a brightly tie-dyed T-shirt in the crowd. There are tie-dye parties, projects at camp, and school art projects using tie-dye. It's fun, it's individual, it's a fashion statement, it's colorful, it's creative, and it's daring. It might even please parents, who may have done some tie-dyeing themselves "in their younger years."

Bright colors are "in" these days. Men's fashions that used to be rather drab, have flourished with colorful ties and bright casual clothing. Women often put a splash of bright color with their business suits to show a little individuality. Kids love bright colors, and putting on a brightly colored outfit gives them a charge of good energy. Teens enjoy making an individual visual statement in their choice of clothing. Besides all of this, color is fun.

In many cultures, it is traditional for the peasants to dress in bright and colorful clothing. The Guatemalan Indians weave beautiful materials for their tribal costumes, each village having its own distinct colors and designs of cloth. The Gypsies of Europe wore bright swirling skirts and beautifully embroidered vests. Japanese kimonos are works of art often incorporating tie-dyed designs known as *tsujigahana*. In Bali, India, and Africa, tie-dye and batik is used to brighten sarongs, saris, skirts, and *dishekis*. The Seminole Indians of Florida sew colorful materials together for their native dress; it's a sign of their tribe. This use of color is their connection to a talented tradition. In these days of economic uncertainty and global friction, clothing can give relief and a healthy diversion, especially clothing that you make yourself and enjoy wearing. The American melting-pot has created its own tribal dress, with tie-dye emerging as an American-crafted art form.

Some people romanticize the 1960s era as a time of idealism, peace, love, and innovation. Tie-dyed clothing is seen as a symbol of those times and is being worn not only for a taste of nostalgia, but as a statement that those ideals still exist.

hat is Tie-Dye?

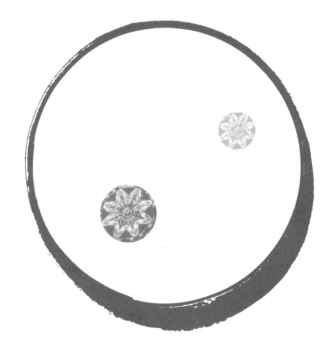

Tie-dye is just what its name implies. The clothing or material is tied and then dyed. Of course, it isn't that simple. Tie-dye is a technique of dyeing using the resist method. Resist is when something like string, rubber bands, wax, clothespins, paper clips, or stitching is used to keep the dye from being absorbed into the material. The resist method creates designs and patterns depending on the placement of the resist materials. The design is also affected by the amount of dye used and where it is placed.

Batik is a cousin of tie-dye. Batik is done by painting or stamping a wax design onto material. The dye does not penetrate the wax and the design shows through, often with interesting lines where the wax has cracked and dye has slipped in. Although this is an interesting art form as well, in this book we are going to be dealing exclusively with tie-dye.

Tie-dye requires a dyeable material which is folded, pleated, or scrunched to create different patterns and designs. These are then tied off with rubber bands or string, or sewn together so the folds don't come apart in the dyeing process. The item can then be dipped or dunked in a dye bath or vat, or dye can be squeezed or dripped onto it. When the ties are removed, the design emerges from where the ties were. A random or specific design can be created depending on how the folding and tying are done. Each part of the process allows for many possibilities, and that's what makes tie-dye so varied and interesting.

istory of Tie-Dye

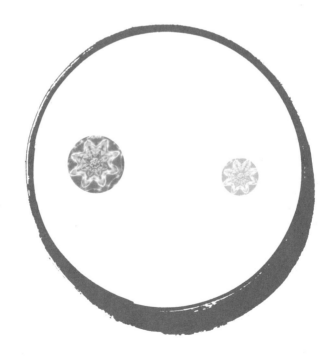

Tie-dye dates back to ancient times. It was one of the ways our ancestors decorated their clothing, along with beads, shells, and other ornamentation. I think back to the story in the Old Testament of the Bible, of Joseph, the son of Jacob. He had a beautiful coat of many colors that was the envy of his brothers. Could it have been tie-dyed?

Tie-dye became fully developed in China during the T'ang Dynasty (618-906 A.D.) and in Japan during the Nara period (552-794 A. D.). The availability of silk and hemp, which are very receptive to the resist technique, made these countries' art outstanding.

Some early tribes in Western China, South East Asia, and Central America tied and dyed the threads before weaving their cloth. When it was woven into material, beautiful designs appeared where the white lines of the tie contrasted with the colored dyes. This method is known as *ikat*.

The colors in the dyes were mostly extracted from roots, flowers, leaves, and berries of plants. These include the blackberry, some species of lichen, safflower, marigold, onion, red cabbage, sage, and a long list of other plants. One of the most popular dyes came from a plant called indigo that makes a beautiful blue dye and is still used today. Some people enjoy the time-consuming process of growing plants and making them into natural dyes. The one problem with these dyes is that over time and in sunlight the colors fade. Today, synthetic dyes have been developed that are permanent, quick-setting, safe, and easy to use, and the colors are ensured by accurate formulas. In this book, we will be using these synthetic dyes, but don't let this stop you from learning about natural dyes. An excellent book, *A Dyer's Manual*, will tell you more about this. (See Bibliography, page 91.)

As in days of long ago, we still use natural fibers for tie-dyeing. The silks from China and cottons from Egypt are still prized, as is the rayon from Bali. Knit cottons made in the United States are our staple. A hemp material made in Hungary and The Netherlands is making its appearance as a durable and dyeable natural fabric.

The tie-dye methods using cotton and silk were passed down in Japan, Indonesia, and Southeast Asia, while cotton and raffia were used in many parts of Africa. Pre-Columbian Peruvians used wool and cotton to make *ikat* designs in their weaving.

In 13th century Japan, tie-dye was a common way of decorating peasants' clothing. Each family could create a little individuality and color in their otherwise hardworking and tedious lives.

From 1568 to 1603, in what's known as the Momoyama period, *tsujigahana* reached its height. *Tsujigahana* is an art combining tie-dye with ornamental drawing using Chinese ink called *sumi*. Tie-dye may be the entire design, or it can be used to create large areas where flowers, landscapes, and trees are drawn into the designs. Traditional dye shops developed new methods for making elegant silk robes.

At that time, Japan was divided into kingdoms that were ruled by warlords. Fighting and raids of one warlord against another were common. The more powerful warlords slowly began taking over their weaker neighbors. Some battles were furious. When an officer of a warlord's army was particularly brave or had won a great victory, the lord would give him gifts of recognition. One of the most prized awards was a tie-dyed kimono or *kosode*. These have been passed down in some families as prized possessions, and many can be found in museums throughout Japan. Over time, the various plant, root, and berry dyes have faded, but the designs of flowers and detailed misty landscapes can still be admired.

These beautiful kimonos exhibit interesting variations in the use of tie-dye. One variation was the creation of a white area by tying off a large piece of the material before dyeing the robe. Then ink would be used to draw pictures on the white area. In another design, rice would be tied into the material in little circles, so that when the material was dipped in blue dye, designs of little white circles would be scattered over the deep blue kimono.

The popularity of tie-dye and the famous dye shops lasted for three hundred years. Eventually the peasants could no longer afford to wear tie-dyed kimonos, but high-society women and their influential and wealthy husbands took pride in wearing these intricate hand-crafted pieces of artwear. The era of the powerful warlords came to an end during the seventeenth century, and the tie-dyed kimono took a back seat, replaced by embroidered cloth from China. However, one can still find shops in Japan that carry on the tradition of tie-dyeing beautiful material.

In Africa ceremonial hats were decorated with tie-dye, as were caftans. In recent years, many local African women have earned money for their families by tie-dyeing material for caftans, shirts, and tablecloths. Many varied styles of tie-dye have emerged to distinguish the different nations of Africa.

In the U.S. during the Roaring '20s pamphlets were printed that gave directions on how to decorate homes with tie-dyed curtains and throw-pillows. We have met several senior women who have told us of making tie-dyes when they were young girls during the Great Depression of the 1930s. They would cut up cotton flour sacks, tie-dye them, and then sew them into clothing, curtains, pillow covers, and tablecloths. When times are rough, tie-dying has been a way to brighten peoples' lives.

Tie-dye came back in style in the 1960s, when a great movement emerged among young people that emphasized individuality. It was time to "do your own thing." Each person could make his or her own statement by tie-dyeing his clothes with this tie or that color combination. Tie-dyed sheets were used as room dividers and wall hangings. Silk and cotton banners were used as backdrops for rock-and-roll concerts.

Since the 1980s, tie-dye has come back into style. It is also slowly being recognized as a highly skilled and sometimes quite difficult and labor intensive art form and craft. Many different colors can now be put on one item to get intricate and detailed designs in brilliant colors. The dyes, which used to fade so badly, have been replaced by dyes that are permanent and easier to use. They can be in bright rainbow colors, or toned down blues, blacks and reds, and earth tones. Pastels are perfect for someone with more conservative tastes. The designs are endless—a spiral, a star, stripes, a bulls-eye, random scrunches, a yoke, a heart, a peace sign, and many more, . . . and each one unique.

Itchiku
Tie-Dye Master

When Itchiku was a young boy growing up in Japan in the 1930s, he worked as an apprentice in a dye house. He learned the ancient techniques and skills of dyeing and tie-dyeing. In Japan, the old ways were revered and apprentices had to start by learning the old ways before they were allowed to branch out and try new ideas and methods.

During World War ll, Itchiku was drafted and sent to Siberia. There he was captured and held in a concentration camp for six years. He kept himself alive and sane by meditating on the beautiful and ever-changing sunsets on the cold Siberian plains. He visualized these sunsets tie-dyed on beautiful silk kimonos. When he was finally released from prison and returned home, he was able to bring his dreams into reality.

Itchiku now runs a famous dye house in Japan where he produces robes of museum quality. He has done a beautiful series of five kimonos of the Siberian sunsets. They start off in brilliant oranges and reds, and as the sun sets, mellow into grays and lavenders and pinks. One can visualize the cold Siberian winters and sense the hope that the colorful sunsets brought to him. Another series of five robes uses water as the theme, with beautiful designs in greens, blues, and aqua.

Itchiku's tie-dye designs are created first by drawing on the silk pieces that make up the kimono. He then sews the designs along the edges and pulls them together. Sometimes a thread will go through only two strands of silk cloth. The method is tedious but the results are exquisite.

After sewing the design, he vat dyes or applies the dyes onto the cloth, steams it, and unties it. He then sews it again on different lines and repeats this process as many as thirty-five times per piece. This gives beautiful shadings of many colors. After the pieces are untied, the different strips of material are sewn together to make the complete kimono. One robe can take up to eight months to complete.

Itchiku's work can be seen in a lovely book titled *Opulence: The Kimonos and Robes of Itchiku Kubota* edited by Tomoyuki Yamanobe (New York: Kodansha, 1984).

 # General Information About Tie-Dying

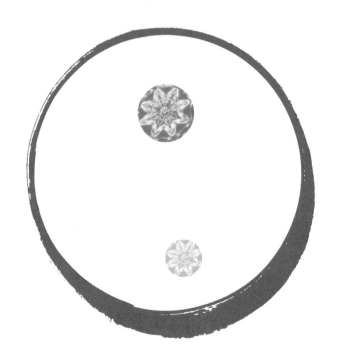

Read over this chapter once
before beginning a tie-dye project.

stage 1
fold & tie

The first step in tie-dyeing is folding and tying the material. This is the essence of the art form. How the folds are made will determine how the design comes out. I have often compared my tying with the Japanese art of paper-folding called *origami*. Detailed folding of the cloth creates intricate patterns. I'm going to discuss some of the easier designs first so that everyone can try them and become familiar with the different results.

To start, soak the fabric to be dyed in a soda ash solution (½ cup soda ash per gallon of water), agitating it for five to ten minutes. Remove the fabric and wring it out thoroughly; the fabric is then ready to fold. Tying cloth soaked in soda ash can be hard on the skin, so use tight gloves that give you dexterity. Surgical gloves are good for this. The right wetness is very important to the final results of the tie-dyed item. If the fabric is too wet, the dye becomes diluted and a washed-out look will result. If the item is too dry, the dye will not penetrate into the cloth and there will be large irregular white areas. If the items are tied dry, they can be dampened before dyeing. To test dampness squeeze the item firmly. There should be no water dripping from it. Wrap string or rubber bands around the design to secure it.

stage 2
dyeing

The next step after folding and tying is dyeing. This is the fun but messy part. It is a good idea to wear old clothes, shoes, and rubber gloves. I love this stage of the process, because here color is the medium. No more all white items!

Although the dye companies can supply you with over seventy colors, I mix most of my own colors. I enjoy mixing dyes that will blend well with other colors to create an overall piece that is pleasing to the eye. Whether the dyes are used straight out of the container or mixed, the results will be exciting. Visualizing the color sequences or drawing them on paper will help one decide how to place the colors. The dye that is made up will look much darker than the final result after the item is rinsed, so adjust the colors accordingly. They may need to be made thicker or thinner, depending on the desired results.

Some colors, when put next to each other, result in a brown or muddy effect. Suppose that the holiday colors of green and red are wanted. These colors will blend into brown at the points where they meet. They must be separated by a section of white or black to make sure the colors remain clean.

Most of the items that I tie have sections tied off with string. Each of these sections can be dyed a different color, or one section can be carefully dyed with several colors. The larger sections that are to remain a solid color, such as the background, can be squirted over a larger container. Be careful to hold the tied sections of the item out of the way so as not to get dye on them. An applicator can be used to get into creases and near the string lines. Squeeze out any excess dye so that it doesn't run up into the tied sections. It's a good idea to hold back the amount of dye used near the string line, because when it is squeezed in, the dye will "creep" more deeply into the material.

Each color of dye has its own personality. Red is what I call a stubborn color. It is thicker and does not flow into the material easily. The folds that are dyed red need to be checked carefully to make sure that the color has penetrated enough. Usually more dye will need to be added.

Yellow is our precious color, and it is easily lost or over-run by other colors. Yellow can always be covered with another color, but once it is lost, there is no getting it back.

Blue, turquoise, green, orange, and black are runaway colors, so they need to be applied carefully with a little room left for them to run, because they will. Orange, a very bright color, can easily run over yellow. In a batch of amateur tie-dyes, the orange is often dominant and garish, so be careful.

Purple, a mix of red and blue, has some of the characteristics of both. It needs to be checked, but tends to absorb pretty well. Purple bleeds a beautiful shade of blue, so it's nice to have some white left in the purple section. Knowledge of the behavior of the individual colors is essential for a balanced and pleasing piece of work.

stage 3
waiting, ugh

After the dyeing process is finished, it is time to play the patience game. This is always the hardest part for the new artist, because it's hard to wait to see the results. There are no one-hour photo labs for tie-dye. The dyes need to set up. The dyes will fix almost 100% in 4 hours at temperatures over 70°F. Cover them with plastic and set them aside to ripen for between 12 and 24 hours (the longer the better). This will give the most "bang" for the dye. The colors will truly be rich instead of faded and washed out.

stage 4
untie

Now it's time to untie and open up the dyed articles. Each one is unique and beautiful. Wear gloves and cut the string or rubber bands *carefully* so as not to cut the cloth. If possible use a scissors with one point blunted for this step.

stage 5
rinse & dry

While still wearing gloves, unfold the material and rinse in lukewarm water until the water is nearly clear. Next wash it in hot water (135-140°F), adding ½ teaspoon of Synthropol® soap per gallon of water (available from the dye companies) to remove the excess dye from the item. Wash in this hot solution for 10 to 15 minutes with good agitation. Remember, in the time the articles were sitting, the dye was combining with the fabric. What is being rinsed out is excess dye that didn't bond. If it is thoroughly rinsed now, it will not run. Add some water softener at this hot water stage so that the items stay soft. For the final rinse, run the items through a warm wash/warm rinse cycle to remove any excess soap and dye. The water should be clear on the final rinse. Squeeze out any excess water. Dry your beautiful creations in a regular dryer or hang them up to dry.

ie-Dyeing
Supplies

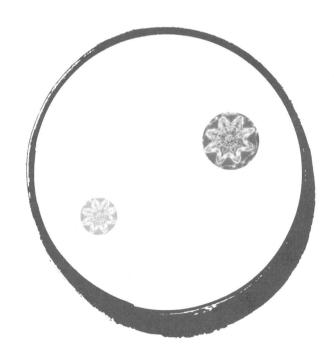

There are several different types of dyes available for tie-dyeing. The dyes available in local grocery stores have been used for many decades. They are inexpensive, but must be used with boiling water. The results often appear faded and are not very permanent.

Another dye, called a "fiber reactive dye," was first developed in the 1950s. This type of dye does not require hot water, and the colors are brilliant and permanent. The molecules of the dye actually combine with the molecules of a cotton, rayon, or silk material to form a strong and permanent bond. These are the dyes that I prefer. They can be purchased at some local craft shops or can be ordered from several dye distributors around the country. (See the listings on page 90.)

The cool-water reactive dyes come under several brand names including Procion®, and Deka Dyes. Some dyes are made for tie-dyeing and batik while others are made for fabric painting. There are dyes that are more applicable to cottons and rayon while others are better for silk. Reactive dyes can only be used on natural fibers including cotton, rayon, hemp, and silk. For best results be sure that the items to be dyed are 100% natural. Although polyester/cotton blends can be dyed, only the cotton in the blend will take the dye and the effect will be muted. In the dyeing and rinsing process the natural fibers will shrink, so when dyeing wearable items be sure to use clothes that are at least a size larger than normal. In normal cotton sheeting items, the shrinkage can be as much as one inch for every six inches of material.

String, rubber bands, clothespins, needle and thread, blocks of wood, rice grains, marbles, and many other items have been used to make the designs of tie-dye. Each gives a unique and interesting effect. This is where experimentation comes in. If tying with string, any weight from kite string to dental floss can be used. If sharp contrasts between white and color in the designs is desired, a strong twine is recommended. It is always helpful to experiment.

Containers, measuring cups, and spoons will be needed to made up the dye. Small plastic containers like cottage cheese or tofu containers are a good size for small amounts of dye, and larger plastic containers are good for dunking large items.

Warning: The dyes are considered relatively nontoxic, but we advise using a respirator and working in a well-ventilated room. Wear rubber gloves that come up as high as possible when mixing and using the dyes. The unmixed dye is a fine powder and repeated inhalation of the powder can cause an allergic reaction in some people. There is a good cleaner, Reduran, that takes dye off of the skin. Keep dye away from the eyes and mouth. Children should be closely supervised when using these dyes. Pregnant and nursing mothers need to be particularly careful with all chemicals. It would be best to discuss this matter with one's doctor before using these dyes. Once utensils and containers have been used for dyes, they should not be used for food.

With minimum precautions and common sense, a safe and enjoyable time can be had.

Applicators are necessary when applying the dye. Many dye companies and craft shops sell squeeze bottles of varying sizes that work well. Eye droppers can also be used to create special effects.

Mixing agents are needed when making up the dyes. Most dye companies supply these with the dyes and have recipes for mixing the dye solution. There are many different formulas that give different results, so some experimenting will be necessary to reach the desired effect.

Even the hardness or softness of the water in a particular region will cause different results, and water softener is often added or decreased to reach the desired formula. When using water softener, use Calgon or Metaphos. Use the proportions listed in the section "Procedure for Mixing Dyes" below.

Some of the chemicals that are used to mix with the dye powders include soda ash, urea, and water softener. Follow the formula as shown below.

Procedure for Mixing Dyes

Mix up a batch of chemical water which can be stored a month or more at room temperature. The chemical water is made by mixing the following ingredients together:

½ cup urea* dissolved in 1 quart soft warm or hot water (If water softener is needed, add 1 teaspoon Calgon or Metaphos.)

Optional: Calsolene oil or Synthrapol may be added to the chemical water, ¼ teaspoon per quart. This helps the dye penetrate the material better.

Pour off the amount of chemical water that is needed for one color. (For ease of measurement, use 1-cup increments.)

Add the dyes in the amount needed for each color as

*Urea may be purchased at a farm chemical supply company or farmer's co-op.

indicated below. (The mix should look darker than the desired color, since some will be washed out in the rinsing process.) Try a pre-dissolved concentrate, add chemical water, and stir until color is right.

> For 1 cup of chemical water (depending on the desired shade), mix:
>> Pale Shade—1 teaspoon dye powder
>> Medium Shade—3 teaspoons dye powder
>> Dark Shade—6 teaspoons dye powder

For deeper shades, particularly the turquoises and blues, the amounts of concentrate may need to be either doubled or quadrupled.

These dyes can be safely poured down the drain.

Don't Forget: Before dying any item, pre-soak and saturate the fabric in a soda ash solution (½ cup ash per gallon of water). Squeeze out any excess liquid. Tie the desired design. Dye the item while it is still wet.

42

 esigns to Try

design 1
accordion fold

This is one of the easiest folds, but also offers many variations. Different variations can result from how large the pleats are, how even each pleat is, and where the pleats are placed on the item. The folds can be placed diagonally, vertically, horizontally, or in a zig-zag stripe. The design can cover the entire item or it can be partially tied so that a solid colored background sets off the design.

Diagonal Stripe Variation

1. To fold the diagonal stripe, divide the shirt in half along the diagonal from the shoulder to the opposite bottom corner of the shirt. (Fig. 1.) Start folding in accordion pleats from the bottom edge of the shirt to the opposite shoulder. (Figs. 2-4.) Try to keep the pleats small and even.

2. Secure the folds with string. (Fig. 5.) Make as many sections as you wish. We made four sections (three tied on both sides, plus one end section). (Fig. 6.)

3. To dye the diagonal stripe, first dye the background a solid color (the loose, untied material at the right of Fig. 6). Try purple, red, or black. Squeeze out any excess dye. Then dye the end section yellow. To guard the yellow, place a little yellow on the second section (the first one tied on both sides). Apply green to the other part of that section. The third secton is turquoise. The fourth section is blue. Over the end of the yellow section, place a little orange and then a little red on the very end of that. (See color Figs. C-1A and C1B.)

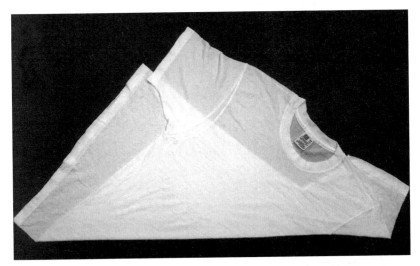

Fig. 1.

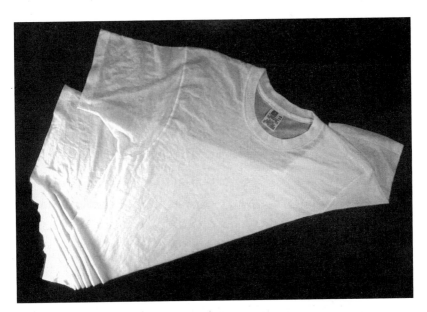

Fig. 2.

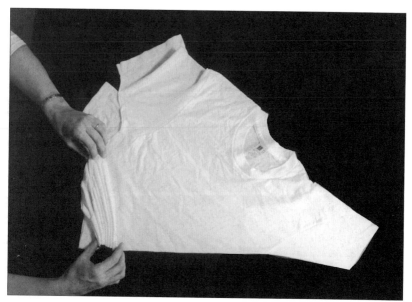

Fig. 3.

Fig. 4.

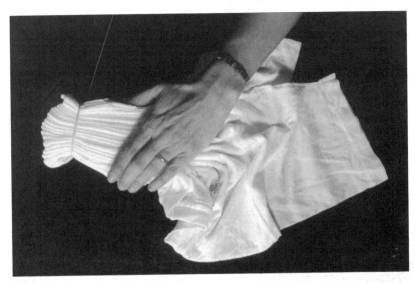

Fig. 5.

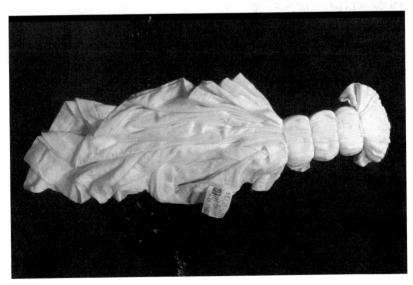

Fig. 6.

Horizontal Stripe Variation

This will give you a horizontal stripe with a background.

1. Fold the shirt in half across the chest. (Fig. 7.) At the fold pleat across the shirt from one side to the other in small, even pleats. (Figs. 8 and 9.)

2. Tie the horizontal stripe in four sections (three tied on both sides, plus one end section—Figs. 10 and 11)

3. To dye the horizontal stripe, first dye the background a solid color (the loose, untied material on the far right of Fig. 11). Try purple, red, or black. Squeeze out any excess dye. Then dye the end section yellow. To guard the yellow, place a little yellow on the second section (the first one tied on both sides) and apply green to the other half. Apply turquoise to the third section. The fourth section is blue. Over the end of the yellow section, place a small amount of orange and then a little red on the end of that.

All-Over Stripe Variation

This will give you several horizontal stripes across the shirt.

1. Fold the shirt in half across the chest. (Fig. 7.) At the fold, pleat across the shirt from one side to the other in small, even pleats. (Figs. 8 and 9.)

2. Tie the horizontal stripe in four sections (three tied on both sides, plus one end section—Figs. 10 and 11), and continue to tie it all the way out to the end of the material for a design that covers the entire shirt. (Fig. 12.)

3. Squirt different colors on each section that is tied. If a rainbow design is desired, place yellow in one of the central sections. Yellow should always be used first in any design, since it is a light color and can easily be taken over by other colors near it. To guard the yellow, place a little yellow on each of the adjacent sections before you apply a darker color. In one direction from the yellow section, dye an orange section, then red, purple, and blue. Many people like blue near the face while some like yellow and red near the face. Decide on the placement of the dye before starting. In the opposite direction from the yellow, apply green, turquoise, blue, and purple on each section in that order, and a beautiful rainbow stripe will appear. If there are more sections, begin the sequence again. (See color Figs. C-1C and C-1D.)

Fig. 7.

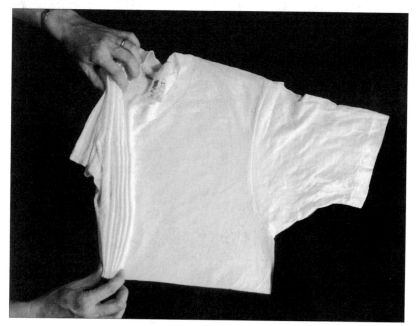

Fig. 8.

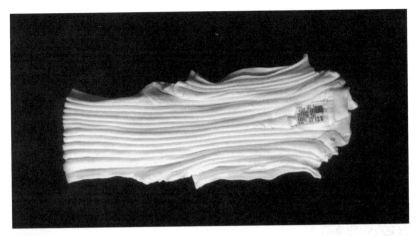

Fig. 9.

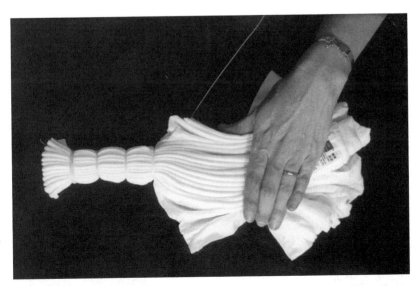

Fig. 10.

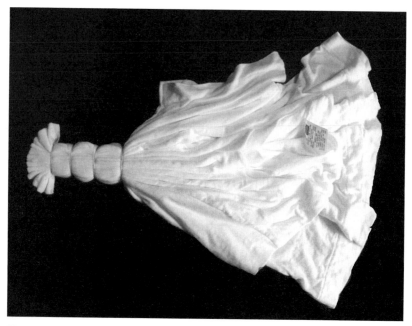

Fig. 11.

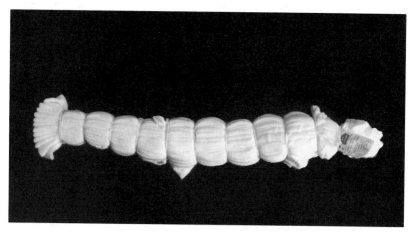

Fig. 12.

design 2
spiral fold

This is one of the most popular designs.

1. To tie the spiral, the middle of the spiral is held down while the rest of the material is swirled around the center. (Figs. 14, 15, and 16.) The middle can be secured with a finger, a stick, or a fork. Again, the accordion fold is being used, but in a circular motion. The care and detail that is given to the folds will result in a more detailed spiral or a more random looking spiral. There is a tendency for the folds to get too big, so each large fold must be divided into two folds as the spiral is being pleated. When the folding is completed, it resembles a mini-pizza, or a party-size pizza if a large item is being tied.

2. Some people tie spirals with rubber bands, but there is more control over the outcome by using string. (Fig. 17.) Tie the spiral securely without losing its circular shape, but not so tightly that it collapses the design. (Fig. 18.)

3. To dye the spiral think of it as a pie. Each color will be a slice of pie. We will describe a rainbow spiral here, but there are an infinite number of color combinations for the spiral that can be substituted. Again, a warning when choosing colors: some will become muddy when placed next to each other. Dye a big slice of the pie yellow, a smaller slice orange, and another larger slice red to make up about half of the pie. The other half, starting next to the red, will be made up of a small purple

section, a large blue one, and a smaller green wedge. We have made the primary colors (yellow, red, and blue) the larger sections and the secondary colors (orange, purple, and green) the smaller sections. An emphasis on primary colors will give a more balanced rainbow effect. Be very careful when applying the dyes close to the middle of the spiral. To be sure that there will be a multi-colored center, don't apply the dyes too closely together. Remember: all the colors, when mixed, become black or brown. (See color Figs. C-2A-2C.)

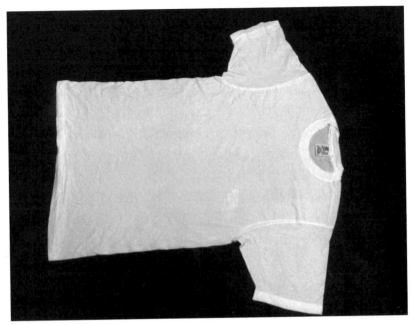

Fig. 13.

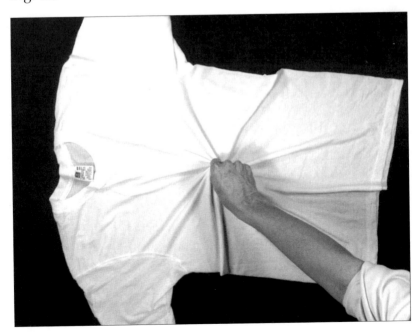

Fig. 14.

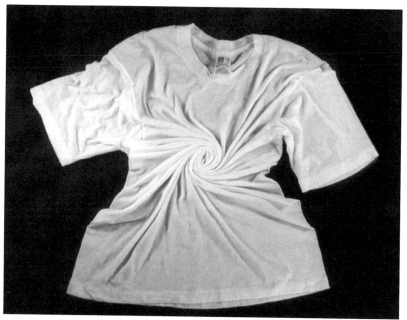

Fig. 15.

Fig. 16.

Fig. 17.

Fig. 18.

design 3
flower fold

1. In this fold, three or four vertical accordion folds are made across the entire item to create one long piece. (Figs. 19, 20, and 21.)

2. The piece is folded in the shape of a triangle and folded back and forth up the entire length of the shirt. (Fig. 22.) Secure this triangle-shaped piece with rubber bands or string to hold it together. (Figs. 23 and 24.) This does not need to be tied too tightly, because of its thickness. The dye must be able to penetrate its many layers.

3. To dye the flower, apply yellow to the sections on each of the left and right corners, as shown in Fig. 24. Make sure the yellow has penetrated the material. Squeeze out excess dye or blot the material with a rag. At the tips of each yellow section, apply an orange section and then a red section on top of the orange, mostly covering the orange. Remember, orange takes over anyway. (See color Fig. C-3B.)

4. Above the yellow section, place a green section and then a turquoise one. The middle section toward the third corner should be blue with purple on the third corner. (See color Fig. C-3C.) In this design, due to the thickness of the fold, the sections need to be checked for too much white and filled in as much as possible. Although an item tie-dyed in this style seems to be filled with dye, the resulting design will still contain a large amount of white. (See color Fig. C-3A.) Blot any dripping dye with a clean rag.

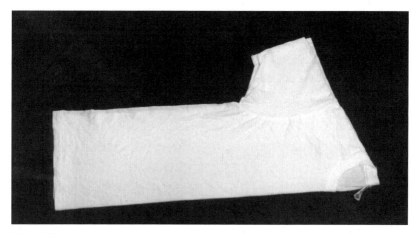

Fig. 19.

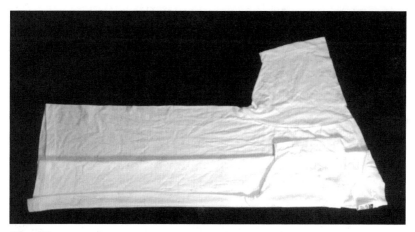

Fig. 20.

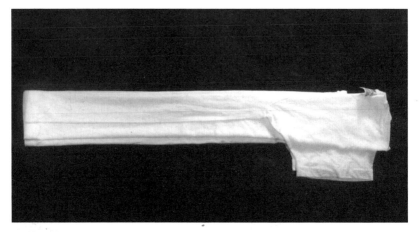

Fig. 21.

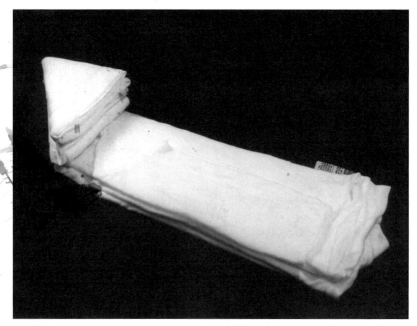

Fig. 22.

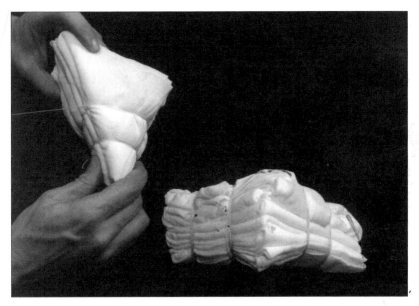

Fig. 23.

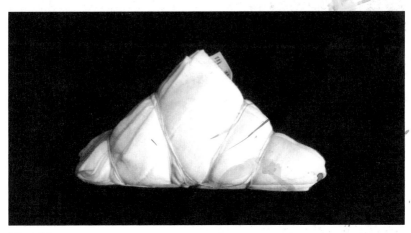

Fig. 24.

design 4
bull's-eye fold

A bull's-eye is a popular design from the '60s. Create one big circle in the middle of your item or lots of little ones all over it. (Figs 25-28)

1. Fold the shirt in half vertically from the middle of the collar to the middle of the bottom hem. Fold in half horizontally by bringing up the bottom of the shirt; one of the corners will now be at the center of the shirt. (Fig. 26.)

2. Fold the shirt like an accordian in an arc from the horizontally folded side to the vertically folded edge. (Fig. 27 and 28.)

3. Grasp the material where the center of the bulls-eye will be and tie it off in sections. (Figs. 29 and 30.) The center can be a large section, if a ring effect is desired. If a target design is wanted, the whole bulls-eye can be tied in smaller sections as in Fig. 30.

4. A loosely tied item will allow more dye to penetrate the cloth. A tightly tied item will leave more white in the design.

5. To dye this design, first pick a color combination. Apply a different color in each section, and squeeze it in well. Try the rainbow color sequence with a yellow center or a blue center, and continue the sequence on the remaining sections: orange, red, purple, blue, and green. If a ring effect is desired, dye the large center section the same color as the background color, with different colors on the tied sections, or leave the tied sections white. (See color Figs. C-4A-C.)

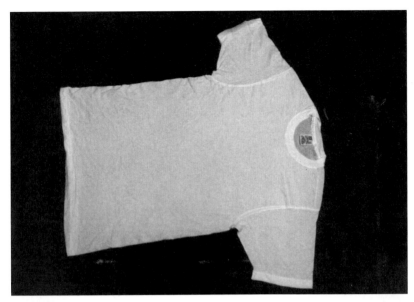

Fig. 25.

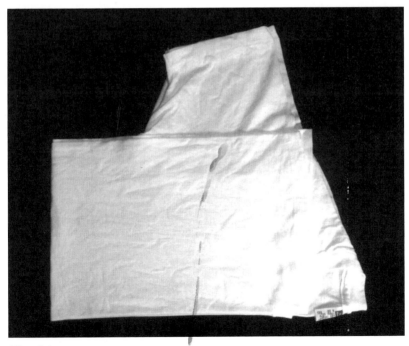

Fig. 26.

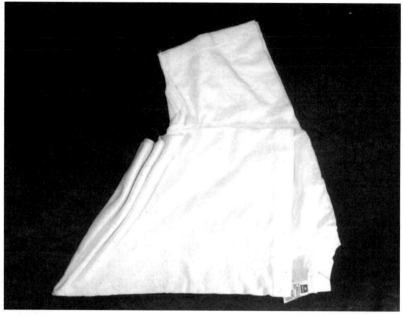

Fig. 27.

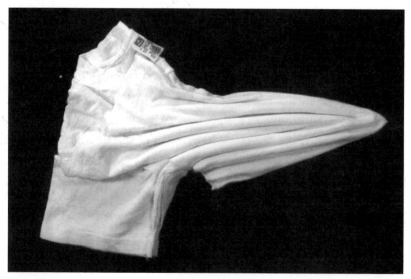

Fig. 28.

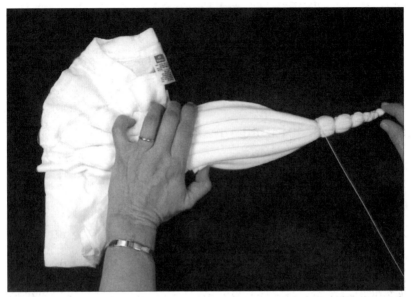

Fig. 29.

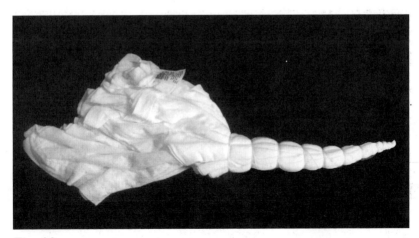

Fig. 30.

design 5
yoke fold

A yoke design is like a necklace. This design can be a shallow necklace or a deep V-shaped design.

1. Fold the shirt in half vertically from the middle of the collar to the middle of the bottom of the shirt. (Fig. 32.)

2. Decide if a deep or shallow yoke is desired. Pick a place on the fold of the shirt, and pleat it from this spot to outside the sleeve seam. (Figs. 33 and 34.)

3. Tie off sections of the yoke in one-inch or two-inch sections. (Figs. 35 and 36.)

4. Dye the background or untied section of this design first. Dip it carefully in a tub of dye, holding the tied design up and away from the dye. It helps to have two people for this step. One can hold the tied design, and one can dunk the background.

5. Squeeze in the dye. Lift the shirt out of the dye and squeeze out the excess dye.

6. The yoke design can be dyed like the stripe or bulls-eye. If the rainbow sequence is desired, start by putting yellow in the middle section. (See color Figs. C-5A-C.)

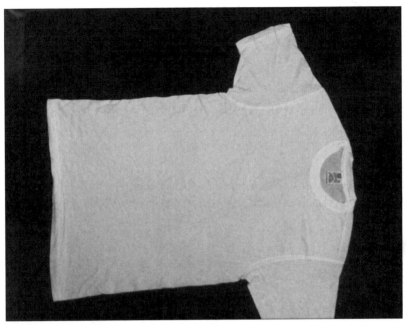

Fig. 31.

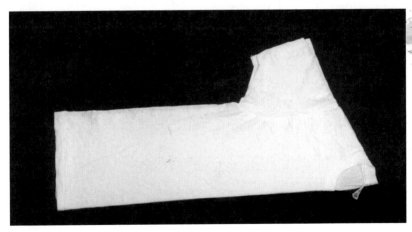

Fig. 32.

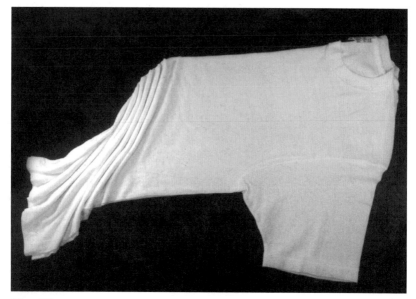

Fig. 33.

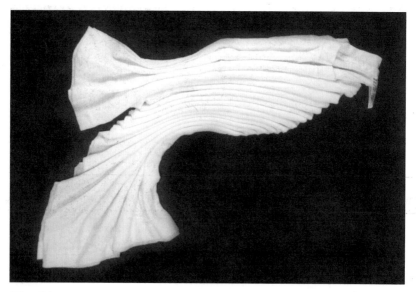

Fig. 34.

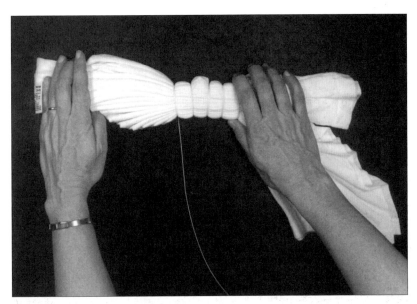

Fig. 35.

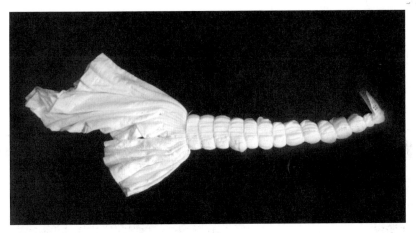

Fig. 36.

design 6
shibori

This is a Japanese method of tie-dyeing that gives a flowing, zebra-striped effect.

1. The Japanese use bamboo. We use wooden dowels or a PVC pipe. Wrap the material around the wood on a diagonal. (Figs. 37, 38, and 39.)

2. Scrunch the material up to one end of the wood. (Fig. 40.)

3. Wrap string around and around the material to secure it there. (Figs. 41 and 42.)

4. Submerge the wood with the material tied on it into a tub of dye, or apply dye to the material with squeeze bottles.

5. After the material has been dunked in the dye and set, untie and rinse. The process can be repeated to add one or more colors. This over-dyeing effect makes for beautiful and unplanned results. The shibori method gives an attractive flair to scarves and pieces of cloth that can later be sewn into clothing. (See color Figs. C-6A-C.)

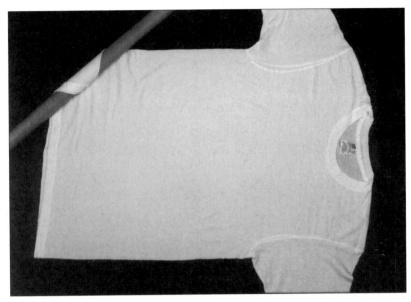

Fig. 37.

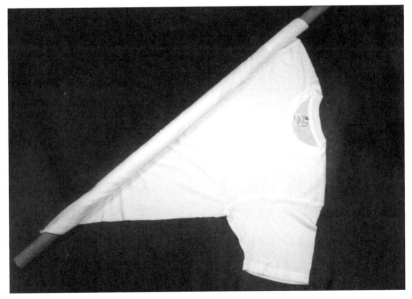

Fig. 38.

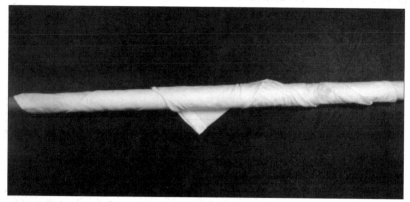

Fig. 39.

Fig. 40.

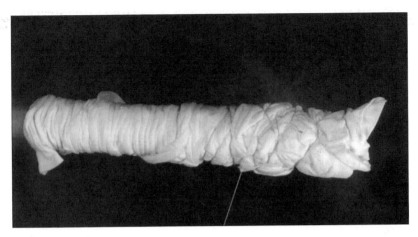

Fig. 41.

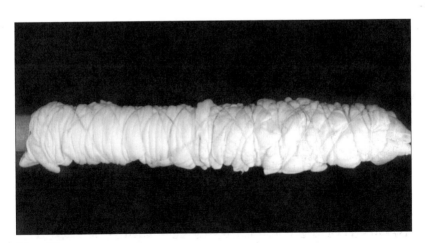

Fig. 42.

design 7
fawn-spot

Another way of tying used by the Japanese is called the "fawn-spot" dyeing method.

1. Small dotted circles are made by wrapping or sewing pinches of cloth at the base with twine before it is immersed in the dye bath.

2. Rice grains can also be sewn into the material in a design or a random pattern. Marbles or other objects can be used to make bigger circles. This is a tedious process if many circles are desired, but it is very intricate and the results are fantastic. (See color Fig. C-7A.) This is an example of Japanese fawn-spot from an antique silk kimono. Notice the spot where the tie came undone during the dye process.

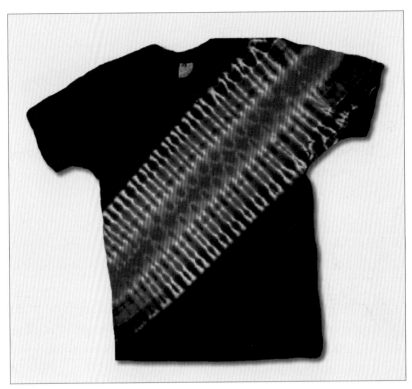

Fig. C-1A - Diagonal stripe, completed

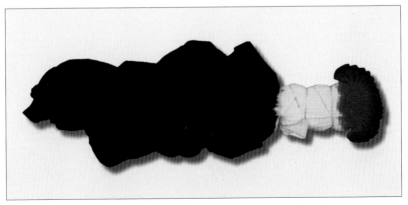

Fig. C-1B - Diagonal Stripe, partially dyed

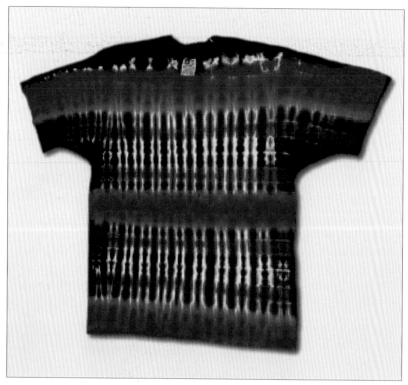

Fig. C-1C - All-Over Stripe, completed

Fig. C-1D - All-Over Stripe, partially dyed

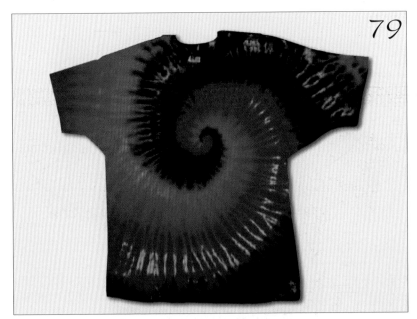

Fig. C-2A - Spiral, completed

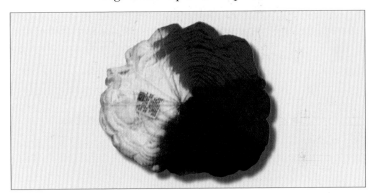

Fig. C-2B - Spiral, partially dyed

Fig. C-2C - Spiral, completely dyed

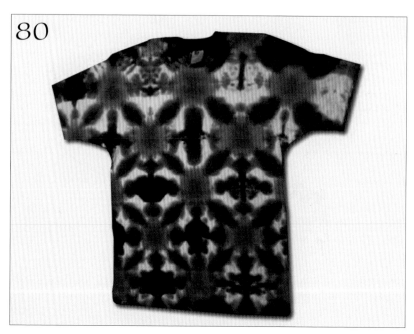

Fig. C-3A - Flower, completed

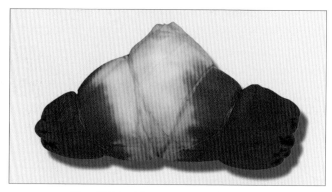

Fig. C-3B - Flower, partially dyed

Fig. C-3C - Flower, completely dyed

Fig. C-4A - Bull's-eye, completed

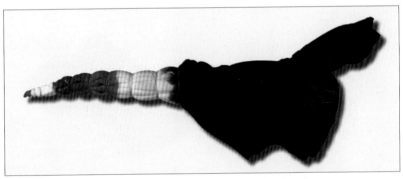

Fig. C-4B - Bull's-eye, partially dyed

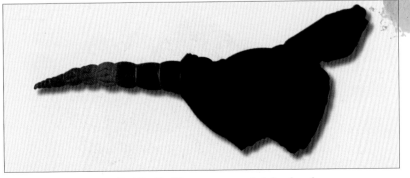

Fig. C-4C - Bull's-eye, completely dyed

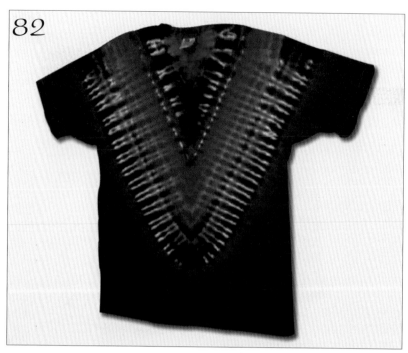

Fig. C-5A - Yoke, completed

Fig. C-5B - Yoke, partially dyed

Fig. C-5C - Yoke, completely dyed

Fig. C-6A - Shibori, completed

Fig. C-6B - Shibori, partially dyed

Fig. C-6C - Shibori, completely dyed

Fig. C-7A - Fawn Dot design on silk

Fig. C-7B - Spiral outfits

Fig. C-7C - Children's clothing, spiral and yoke designs

Fig. C-8A - Advanced designs by professional dyers at Harmony
Enterprises: shooting star and mandala yoke.

Fig. C-8B - Advanced design by professional dyers at Harmony
Enterprises: Quilt with sixteen mandalas

Fig. C-8C - Advanced design by professional dyers at Harmony
Enterprises: Wallhanging with eight-point mandala.

Conclusion

The designs described in this book are a few ideas on which to begin. Let your imagination take it from here! Some of these designs can be combined. The inner artist in all of us takes over and creates original patterns and methods.

After the pieces of art are completed, the job of art critic comes into play. This is the time to really see what has been created, what is pleasing, and what needs improvement. How did the designs turn out, the placement of color, the color sequence? To be a serious artist and improve your techniques, take notes for the next tie-dye session. Otherwise it is easy to forget what to change and what to keep the same. By doing this, the work will show great improvement, and there will be much satisfaction in mastering this complicated and intricate art form. The fascinating thing about tie-dye is that each piece comes out unique and individual. The public is beginning to become aware of the skill needed to tie-dye and will appreciate any effort.

I hope this book will provide many enjoyable experiences creating tie-dyed artwear and furnish an understanding of the intricacy and finesse of this ancient art form.

SOURCES FOR DYES

Dharma Trading Co.
P.O. Box 150916
San Rafael, CA 94915
1-800-542-5227
e-mail: catalog@dharmatrading.com
www.dharmatrading.com

Harmony Enterprises
512 14th Street
Modesto, CA 95354
1-209-571-2767
www.harmonytie-dyes.com
(to order tie-dyes, dye kit, and book)

PRO Chemical and Dye Co.
P.O. Box 14
Somerset, MA 02726
1-800-2BUYDYE
www.prochemical.com (more dyeing instructions)

Rupert, Gibbon and Spider, Inc.
P.O. Box 425
Healdsburg, CA 95440
1-800-442-0455

BIBLIOGRAPHY

Dharma Trading Co. *Fiber Arts Supplies Catalog*. San Rafael, CA: Dharma Trading Co., 1994.

Goodwin, Jill. *A Dyers Manual*. London: Palham Books, 1982.

Museum of Contemporary Crafts of the American Crafts Council. *Fabric Vibrations: Tie and Fold-Dye Wall Hangings and Environments*. New York: Museum of Contemporary Crafts of the American Crafts Council, 1972.

Shaw, Robin and Jennifer. *Batik: New Look at an Ancient Art*. New York: Doubleday and Co., 1974.

Toshiko Ito, Tsujigahana. *The Flower of Japanese Textile Art*. Tokyo: Kodansha International, 1981.

Yamanobe, Tomoyuki, ed. *Opulence: The Kimonos and Robes of Itchiku Kubota*. New York: Kodansha International USA Ltd., 1984.

Dye notes and mixing formulas:

Dye notes and mixing formulas: